NATIONAL
GEOGRAPHIC

All Kinds of Maps

Stevie Prince

You can learn a lot about a place
by looking at a map.
Different kinds of maps show
different things.

This is a political map of the United States.
It shows how people have divided the land
into 50 states.
Two of the states are not connected
to the others.

ALASK

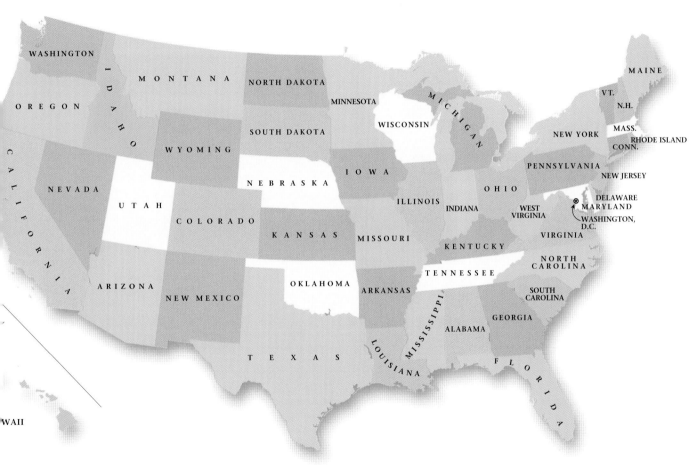

WASHINGTON

OREGON

IDAHO

MONTANA

NORTH DAKOTA

MINNESOTA

SOUTH DAKOTA

WYOMING

WISCONSIN

MICHIGAN

MAINE

VT.

N.H.

NEW YORK

MASS.

RHODE ISLAND

CONN.

CALIFORNIA

NEVADA

UTAH

COLORADO

NEBRASKA

IOWA

ILLINOIS

INDIANA

OHIO

PENNSYLVANIA

NEW JERSEY

DELAWARE

MARYLAND

WASHINGTON, D.C.

WEST VIRGINIA

VIRGINIA

ARIZONA

NEW MEXICO

KANSAS

MISSOURI

KENTUCKY

TENNESSEE

NORTH CAROLINA

OKLAHOMA

ARKANSAS

SOUTH CAROLINA

TEXAS

LOUISIANA

MISSISSIPPI

ALABAMA

GEORGIA

FLORIDA

WAII

5

This is a physical map of the United States. It shows physical features of the land such as mountains and rivers.

mountain

river

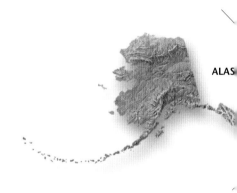

ALAS

HAWAII

Physical Features

- Mountain
- Desert
- Lake or river
- Ice and snow

7

This is a population map of the United States.
It shows which parts of the country are
most populated.
Some places have a lot more people
than others.

lots of people

a few people

ALASK

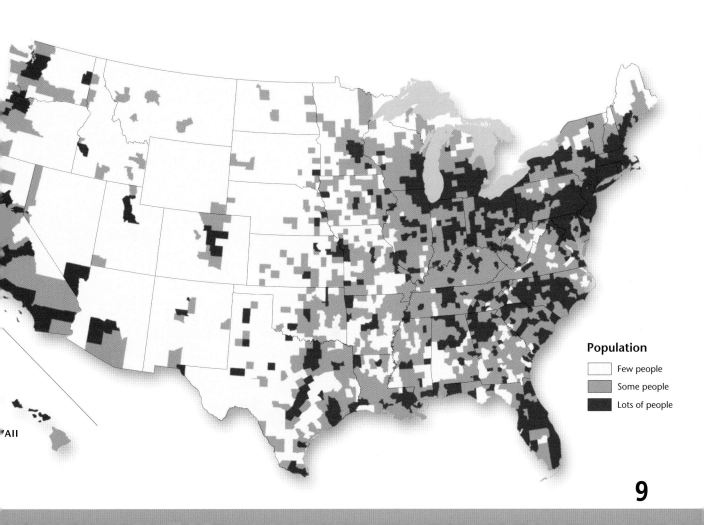

Population

- Few people
- Some people
- Lots of people

All

9

This is a climate map of the United States.
It shows what the climate is like in different parts
of the country.

very cold

very dry

ALASKA

CLIMATE ZONES

- Wet
- Dry
- Mild
- Warm summers, cold winters
- Very cold
- High mountains

HAWAII

11

This is a land use map of the United States. It shows how the land is used in different parts of the country.

farmland

wetland

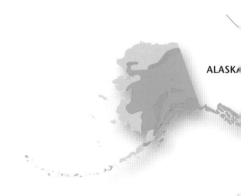

ALASKA

LAND USE

- Barren land
- Farmland
- Farmland and forest
- Forest
- Grazing land
- Tundra
- Urban land
- Wetland

HAWAII

13

This is a road map of the United States.
It shows where the major highways in the country
are located.

ALASKA

interstate highway

Interstate highway

WAII

Index